AF489699

Dream Tree

Haiku by David Watts

Cyberwit.net
HIG 45 Kaushambi Kunj, Kalindipuram
Allahabad - 211011 (U.P.) India
http://www.cyberwit.net
Tel: +(91) 9415091004
E-mail: info@cyberwit.net

Printed at Repro India Limited.

tall sky
near the center of the forest
a dream tree

cold snap
on the blackened branch
a folded owl

in my head
the songs he used to sing
my brother's grave

summer honey
the sweetness
clover kept

her deliberate answer
the shaped silence
of a bonsai

dog day afternoon
a dragonfly drops circles
on the pond

the oboe of longing
between her lips
the reed sings

rainfall
bits of river
in the sky

the ant runs this way
and that   this way—
make up your mind

dam removed
the river
feels its way

my dying cat
memories of tree-climbing
in the curling of her paws

away from my warm bed
the rooms have conspired
with winter

the elm
has a name
but it is not elm

windy beach
sunset in the fold
of a wave

ripples on the mere
the line
of the wind's edge

bone moon
no coins
at the bottom of his cup

father aging
the turn of the beach
at land's end

the view of sunlight
through water
his ashes in the pond

rain over sea
she links her arm
in mine

polar shift
I sway outside
myself

altered reality
the swan's wake
ripples the trees

rearview mirror
the woman
I never should have loved

congressional hearing
the gavel
loses its grip

barn dream
picking sparkles of hay
from her hair

first amnion kick
a curled fish
unfolding

potato sprouts
my son asks
about reincarnation

I see only sky
geese
a flight path

my empty wallet
the homeless man
wishes me well

tight alley
laundry talk
at the windows

echo cannot speak mountain snow

family travel
to Colorado
we meet ourselves

neighbor's new fence
my roots
under his ground

morning fog
the shape
of fog

first the mountain
then the valley
morning light

places
my father took me
river mountain sky

sun slips under a cloud
think I'll borrow an apple
off my neighbor's tree

hazy morning
she stirs a memory
in her cup

above the cliff
my shadow
over the edge

silver moon
the coyote swells to the edge
of his wail

thunder
a pod of grackles
explodes the tree

sun on winter pond
ice and water
dissolving boundaries

rain the shape of the fallen pine

her face
ignites goes out ignites
passing firefly

desert night
stars
touching the horizon

San Gabriel River
our teenage love
occasionally deep

eve of the storm
the forest draped
in silence

still waters
the jagged edge
of the loon cry

bell tower
secrets
on a plaster wall

footprints
the shape
of her leaving

candlelight
rosebud vase
table for one

thread of moon
sliver of soap
in the dish

alphorn
what the mountain
gives back

fireplace glow
the tender margins
of her nightgown

my hospital bed
the out of doors
on my father's coat

nothing more to do winter

freezing midnight mass
no fuzz
on the boy's pure notes

deeper tones
as the milking bucket fills
morning frost

seed kite in the stairwell
not enough wind
to go upstairs

winter mountain hut
the burn of gluhwein
in my throat

mist rises
from moon-weighted wetlands
deep autumn

a glow of stillness
egret on the marsh
at twilight

early morning insomnia
the constellations
out of sorts

the frenetic scurry
of tiny ants
a crumb if I had one

his best stories
the way
they never were

the model's pose
nothing moving
but her eyes

chalkboard
his mathematical solution
in the arrangement of dust

this year
I need more layers
barbed wire wind

lantern glow
the bed sheets soften
in shadow

quiet moon
the mouse escapes
the owl

sudden rain
her yard puddle
hooks up with mine

moon on water
sunlight
twice reflected

candle flame
feet tied down
still it dances

sudden wind
a squall of fallen leaves
down the alley

warm snickerdoodles
another kid comes down
from the tree

cottonwood tufts
brushstrokes
in the wind

mother tree
daughter saplings
what we do not hear

after rain
a thousand sparkles
live oak

seven birches
the wind has something
for each

Acknowledgments:

Gratitude for the editors who chose these poems and for the literary magazines that published them.

Honors

Irish Haiku Society International Contest: "thunder"   Honorable Mention

Haiku Poets of Northern California   International Haiku Contest: "above the cliff"   Honorable Mention

The Iris Little Haiku Contest, Croatia: "the river"   Commendation

The Haiku Crush Best Haiku Anthology: "the beauty of her face"

Publications

Frogpond: "desert night"   "his best stories"

Heron's Nest: "rain the shape"

The Zen Space: "the oboe of longing"

Hedgerow: "first the mountain"   "nothing more to do"   "places"

Modern Haiku: "seed kite in the stairwell"

Creatrix: "in my head"   "the ant runs"

Taj Mahal: "morning fog"

Autumn Moon: "mist rises"

Akitsu Quarterly: "thread of moon"   "candlelight"

The Bamboo Hut: "dusk"

Human/Kind: "neighbor's fence"

Under the Basho: "echo cannot speak"   "a glow of stillness"

Bottle Rockets: "deeper tones"

Haiku Universe: "away from my warm bed"

Spelt Virtual Christmas Advent Calendar Dec 24: "freezing midnight mass"

Better Than Starbucks: "bell tower" "still waters"

tsuri-doro: "the eve of the storm"

Red Alder Review: "sun on winter pond"

Wales Haiku Journal: "this year" "my dying cat" "my hospital bed"

Lyrical Passion: "winter mountain hut"

Presence: "the model's pose"

Alba: "early morning insomnia"

Kokako: "sun slips under a cloud"

Mariposa: "chalkboard" "lantern glow"

Cattails: "silver moon

I am indebted to Carolyn Hall for suggestions about the selection of haiku for this book.